BECKETT SOUNDINGS

OTHER BOOKS
BY INGE ISRAEL

Reflexions
(St.Germain-des-Prés, 1978)

Même le soleil a des taches
(St.Germain-des-Prés, 1980)

Aux quatre terres
(Vermillon, 1990)

Raking Zen Furrows
(Ronsdale, 1991, Japanese translation, 2007)

Unmarked Doors
(Ronsdale, 1992)

Le tableau rouge
(Vermillon, 1997)

Rifts in the Visible / Fêlures dans le visible
(Ronsdale, 1997)

BECKETT
Soundings

POEMS

To Stefanie and John
with love
Inge

inge israel

RONSDALE PRESS

BECKETT SOUNDINGS
Copyright © 2011 Inge Israel

RONSDALE PRESS
3350 West 21st Avenue
Vancouver, B.C., Canada V6S 1G7
www.ronsdalepress.com

Typesetting: Julie Cochrane, in New Baskerville 11 pt on 13.5
Cover Image: John Haynes/Lebrecht Music & Arts Photo Library
Cover Design: Julie Cochrane
Paper: Ancient Forest Friendly Silva — 100% post-consumer waste, totally
    chlorine-free and acid-free

Ronsdale Press wishes to thank the following for their support of its publishing program: the Canada Council for the Arts, the Government of Canada through the Canada Book Fund, and the Province of British Columbia through the Book Publishing Tax Credit Program and the British Columbia Arts Council.

Library and Archives Canada Cataloguing in Publication

Israel, Inge
    Beckett soundings / Inge Israel.

ISBN 978-1-55380-112-2

    1. Beckett, Samuel, 1906–1989 — Poetry. I. Title.

PS8567.S73B43 2011   C811'.54   C2010-907535-8

At Ronsdale Press we are committed to protecting the environment. To this end we are working with Canopy (formerly Markets Initiative) and printers to phase out our use of paper produced from ancient forests. This book is one step towards that goal.

Printed in Canada by Marquis Book Printing, Quebec, Canada

With my love to Werner,
ever ready to listen, to sympathize,
to find and lug home volume after
heavy volume for my research,
and to Pia, Ralph, Allie and Sive who
were unfailingly encouraging
throughout the process.

Last but not least
with love to the memory
of Mark's shining spirit and
unbelievable fortitude.

ACKNOWLEDGEMENTS

My deepest gratitude to Ronald Hatch,
who first suggested the idea for a book
on Samuel Beckett and without whose
staunch, ongoing support and interest
it would never have happened.
My thanks also to Romany, a tireless
cheerleader for believing it could be done,
and to Deborah Trayhurn, whose warm
empathy and insightful comments
were a great comfort.

CONTENTS

Introduction

—

Life under an autocratic regime often singles out people of a strong and defiant temperament and nurtures their talents. Survival under oppression gives them a special character. Samuel Beckett somehow fits this mould although his preoccupations were apolitical. His concern was the cruelty of life itself and his dissatisfaction was directed at the whole of creation.

Arguably the pre-eminent avant-garde writer of the twentieth century, Beckett presents many glaring paradoxes. His being born in a country ruled by the Catholic Church yet raised by a strict and devoutly Protestant mother honed his rebellious spirit on two fronts at once. He loved the King James Bible and knew long passages of it by heart but did not believe in it. He loved his mother but fought to free himself of her until well into his middle years. He loved Ireland but left to live in France. His elite education and extraordinarily retentive memory of all he read and admired were, he felt, an impediment to his own writing..He had a deep urge to write yet despaired of language being able to express anything meaningful. He dearly loved to be in the company of close friends yet remained a solitary man, almost misanthropic. In a way, he was the ultimate rebel.

An insatiable reader, Samuel Beckett was passionate about the classics, ancient literatures and art as well as music, and also fascinated by mathematics. He filled several notebooks with witty or otherwise memorable phrases or sentences that he came across, which he later wove into the fabric of his own writing. However, at a certain point, he began to rebel against verbosity, not least in the writing of his mentor, James Joyce, much as he continued to admire him. From then on he went to unimaginable lengths to condense his own writing until only the barest essence of his thought is left for us to decipher, though the sound of the words, their music and rhythm remain all-important.

His amazing feat of distillation and the many contradictions of his life aroused my curiosity and sent me on a journey of discovery to search for some of the avenues and conduits he may have followed. Having grown up in France and Ireland myself — Beckett's two countries — would, I hoped, help me. The poems in this book are the fruits of my search and my interpretation of the findings.

If, while exploring Beckett terrain, I have succeeded here and there in capturing a winged thought which might have been his in the making, or the seed of an idea where and how it first germinated, nothing could be more gratifying. It is my fervent hope that he would not have been offended by my attempts at understanding him. Even if, at times, I have allowed myself to be carried away by my enthusiasm and fascination, I hope he might have found it in his heart to forgive me. By all accounts he could be very stern with intruders, but was of a generous nature.

*To think, when one is no
longer young, when one is not yet
old, that one is no longer young,
that one is not yet old, that is
perhaps something.*

— SAMUEL BECKETT

—

*Thoughts are the shadows
of our feelings — always
darker, emptier, and simpler.*

— FRIEDRICH NIETZSCHE

They Don't Tell You

when you're born
that you're not really
born, not completely,
not all of a piece,
that the rest of you lags
behind, far behind
like the tail of a comet
trailing in ancient history.

Personne ne nous apprend

quand on vient au monde
qu'on ne naît pas vraiment
pas entièrement
qu'on n'est pas intact
qu'une partie de nous traîne
derrière tout au loin
comme la queue d'une comète
dans l'histoire ancienne.

Betwixt

I said my prayers nightly
long ago, in Sandycove,
on my knees
Mother above me
willing me not to be
a sinner

Father below in the water
of the Gentlemen's Only
at the Forty-foot
urging me to dive in
from the rocks through
the air, arms outstretched
as I'd done from the high
branches of a tree
when I fell on my face,
as I still do in nightmares,
dive in close to where
Joyce rose
from his Tower nodding
to the "snot-green sea,
the scrotum-tightening
sea — our mighty mother."

The "Forty-foot" is a celebrated swimming hole among the rocks in Sandycove, at that time, exclusively for men to bathe in naked.

It All

March. "No flies about today,"
quips the conductor, rubbing
red-cold hands as we board
his bus at St. Stephen's Green,
then catches sight of the woman
in shortish skirt heading straight
for the spiral staircase, and strains
forward to see under it as she mounts,
still rubbing his hands. "Ach,
you've no shame in you at all!"
smirks another, winking,
voice congratulatory.

Never done revolving
it all, Mother would not
wink but promptly swat
the first spring fly
before its compound eye
could spot another,
never mind mount it
or be mounted.

It All *was the original title of* Footfalls, *a Samuel Beckett play.*

An Aching

When I think about loss
it's my father I mourn,
gentle, modest, slow
at the last, pretending
to stop to look
at something

if only I'd been a better
son, a different son
walking hand in hand
then side by side
under brooding clouds
along the shore he loved
or up the Glencullen road
over mountain slopes
the sea slowly coming
into view, at night alive
with lights flashing
and dancing around
Dun Laoghaire harbour

in his presence feeling
a warmth, an aching
I could not voice, feeling
like a man not a man
reared as a child
that died
and did not die.

St. Kevin's Tower, Glendalough

an Irish legend

It rises, hardened ecstasy
amid ancient tombstones leaning
in adoration. Tangled brambles
guard the opening where refugees
once clambered up, pulling
their ladders after them
to the clang of sword on sword
and Viking shouts that shook
the hills. Deep power lives
on in old ruins squatting
in thick greenness.

Here, in a hollow trunk, Kevin hid
from Kathleen's implacable passion
saw lark flames dart about
stained-glass trees shed light
then pushed her into the lake
to become one with virgin clay
and he a saint.

Many have come here to worship,
to learn about sainthood
in the glow that weaves heaven
with earth and earth
with fathomless depths

while Kathleen's moans rise
from the lake, mourning
her love and all the world's
lost love.

But I, no saint, only
the creature your savage loving
made me, could not dodge
yours, Mother.

Lesson

Bleak daylight turns tough
green gorse into relentless
yellow, lighting up
the landscape
where I learned what
I know about men
the way they have
of putting up with it
and swore I wouldn't

learned also
that many's the man
who lost much just because
he missed the chance
to say nothing.

At the Grand Canal, Dublin

There she is, close to where
I first saw her, near Portobello
Bridge. Along the canal whores
stretch their legs. As before
she puts down her bundle
where the grass grows
sparse and grey like hair
on old men's chests,
crosses herself,
wearily picks it up,
takes a step, puts it down,
crosses herself again,
repeats the same sequence
over and over, mouthing
a prayer I cannot catch
seeking solace
in the ritual itself
or in the moments
of lightness felt
at each shedding
of her worldly burden,
the only one that can be.

Of Treatments

Rest! they tell those
who cough out their hearts
in the Home for the Incurable.
Rest, remember it is better
to be seated than upright,
lying down
rather than seated

rest! — enough to ease
into the next world.

How it Was

In the Irish sky outside
my room, I'd see the sun,
a prize-fighter's bloodshot
eye, peer through a slit
of swollen cloud and highlight
the black cross rising past
my window: a magpie, tail
trailing, wings outspread,
an ominous white dot on each,

rise past alder branches
drooping with jaundiced
leaves — clusters of overripe
forgotten grapes
soon trampled
to bitter mud

how far from the clusters
of grapes in Solomon's
song — young breasts
for a brief time,
his headrest.

On Writing

Pushed to the last
bloody ditch
what can you do but sing?

Sing. Yes.

Must find the voice, must dig
for those notes, deep
in dark, weedy waters,
draw out a sound
itself dispassionate
but triggering passion,
laughter, tears, just
as mating frogs, in their frenzy,
bring forth from tiny throats
the mighty song of songs,
the most ancient of all

so true
I will leave no maggot lonely.

Style

My writing stinks of Joyce.
Why does only his way
interest me? His weak voice
— oh how deceptive!
It marshals every available
force, culminates
in a powerhouse of language
and his own convictions. He *is*
the greatest, heir to Shakespeare,
without the shadow of a doubt,
has always known it, since well
before he wrote a thing

ought to get the Nobel, deserves it!
In thrall to his voracious appetite
for words, for puns, he laps up
everyone else's too, must if he is
to fill gargantuan volumes, the most
unread literary masterpieces
of all time.

Could I out-Joyce him? Perhaps
not, being prey to endless doubts.
What matter? The world cannot bear
more than one such maelstrom.

The Catastrophic Eye

Eyes lead a double life
— there's the vulnerable eye
of the flesh that breathes,
sees all too clearly,
devours, and digests,
the "vile jelly" that Cornwall
gouges in *Lear*

while the other, the inner eye
needs no light to attract
imaginings into itself and swell
to disastrous proportions
— like a white dwarf that pulls
gas from its bloated neighbour,
grows into a supernova
and ends as a catastrophe.

Götterdämmerung

Moments before the great
conflagration consumes heaven
and earth, the precious ring
rescued just in time for the whole
unfortunate cycle to begin again,
Wagner's Siegfried, about to fight
Fafner, the dragon, lies on his back
in the depths of a forest when,
prodded either by its leafy murmurs
or by the sound of a distant hunting
horn, he wonders how his mother
looked and why he cannot recall her.
You and your symbols, Wagner!
and your little birds of meaning . . .

though it's true enough, at such
moments the mind harks back
to when the gift of life
is forced down one's gullet
and one begins the solo flight
as if it were possible to reverse
as if one were not in a spot
where one can neither be
what one is nor become
what one could be.

Jack B. Yeats

His solitary figures set against
an alien landscape touch me
the hints of cruel humour
the emptiness invoked in waste
and sky, the compelling particulars
captured in a few deft strokes
showing the impassable immensity
between solitude that cannot quicken
into loneliness and loneliness
that cannot lapse into solitude

not that I'm blind to his romantic
view of peasants and fishermen
portrayed with a Celtic optimism
I cannot accept
yet can never quite deny . . .

and his *Morning*! Almost skyscape,
wide street leading into Sligo
with a boy on a horse
. . . always morning and a setting out
without the mourning
of coming home.

---

*One of the 20th century's most important figures in the visual art of Ireland,
Jack Butler Yeats painted scenes of daily Irish life and Celtic mythology which
contributed to the surge of nationalist spirit in Irish painting after the War of
Independence. Beckett, though very poor, bought* Morning *from Yeats.*

The Battle of Jericho

How to free myself from
the bane of learning?
It clutters up my every
thought. Texts I know by heart
spring to mind unbidden,
word for word! How to cast
off the straightjacket
of canonical immersion,
eradicate borrowings,
allusions, before they creep
into my work, incurring ever
greater debt to an intellectual
tradition I'm dismantling
to the last crumbling stone
while retaining — aye,
there's the rub — nostalgia
for its values.

Must work harder
on ineffable impotence.
It hasn't been properly
exploited.

It's a Poor Memory that Only Works Backwards

The play that cannot be
written is unlike the one not
written and those abandoned
— waifs dropped surreptitiously
by the roadside on a foggy night
in the secret hope they may
miraculously find legs or, better
still, wings

while we toss about in bed
and hear all we hoped
forgotten scream
in our dreams.

The title is a phrase of Lewis Carroll's.

Code

I've tried to live by your four-rule
méthode, Descartes: to accept
as true only what is presented
so clearly as to exclude all doubt;
divide difficulties into their smallest
parts; order thoughts according
to complexity, beginning
with the simplest; make
enumerations so complete
as to omit nothing.

From this code, you claimed
in good faith an outline so clear
and rational emerges, it leads
straight to the knowledge of God.

Well, my friend, I've tried this path.
It leads straight to the depths below.

The Fate of Stars

Those countless new stars
being born in distant galaxies
look strangely vulnerable,
each a bald head in its surround
of blood-red gases, about
to embark on an existence
if not a life, oblivious
of the course ahead,
the violence and destruction,
the imposed restrictions
and, though it will be stuck
in the same one for millennia,
no say in any aspect
of its own orbit
nor in the choice of a partner

not that these are predetermined,
though the damn patterns are
created by laws of physics
that must be obeyed
or there'd be nothing
but collisions and we can't
have that. Tidiness
above all things! even
in the theory of chaos.

Perceptions

In Leibniz's view,
the "little world" is
a microcosm of the big world
and, as in a mirror image,
each reflects the other's
laws of perfect proportion
and Leibniz saw
that it was good

while Schopenhauer saw
us hold a small brooding
world in our brain
a tiny human consciousness
that alone apprehends
the enormous universe

he did not need to add
"with all its imperfections."
We know he knew
it was not good.

Coming to Go

Your mother may not have
meant to have you, may
have done all she could
not to have you, but there
you are, one fine day,
unasked, body, limbs
head in place, tongue
in working order with no
say but, even if you had,
what is there to say
so you want to say nothing
yet fill up the silence
as if it were an obligation
before exiting the great
"cunt of existence."

Charles Baudelaire

"*Hypocrite lecteur,*" you said, "*mon
semblable, mon frère!*" Clever insights,
Monsieur Baudelaire. You too had great
passion for art, for language,
were haunted by the misery
and suffering you saw; gloomy
as hell, abhorring the pus
of the world's abscesses; repulsed
by its stink; condemned
for obscenity; feeling each passing
second ejaculate memories,
nightmares, anger, even neuroses.
But there end the similarities.
Kindred souls we are not

yet a tableau turns this weary day
into an event: your send-up
of bourgeois obsession with
immorality by taking a "five-franc
whore" where she'd never been,
the Louvre and, before immortal
masterpieces, sculptures and paintings,
seeing her blush, squirm with shame,
try to pull you away by your sleeve,
asking how could anyone publicly
display such obscenities.

Van Gogh

"Writing is actually an awful way
to explain things to one another,"
he wrote to Theo, with the same
clear-sightedness and exasperation
he felt while pushing with
his brush against the limits
of what can be rendered.

He saw crows, black wings
extended, become dark
crests on hungry sky-surf
eyeing pleading corn below,
or desperate black smiles
on mucus-cloud.

The vision flowed
from his fingertips, hardened,
gave brief respite, a quiet
just long enough for him to sit
once more listening to inner
voices before the church
without a door, where choices
are made, where the road
divides in two, one side leading
to uncertain life, the other
to a dubious grave.

"When you think he never sold a single canvas!" Beckett said.

Doors

In the heart of the Vieux Marais,
I see a woman emerge from a discreet
doorway, furtively look about
before zipping cash into a bag
then quickly walk away as if
she'd never seen that door

the same one Rodin went through
to pawn a hand from one
of his own sculptures

the same once opened
by Victor Hugo's mistress
sent to raise a loan

mornings, down-and-outs of Paris
dragged their mattresses
through it for a few centimes
to last the day, "earned" some
to retrieve them at night
and sleep near métro vents
spewing stinking warmth

all of us mere blobs on a huge
canvas — as Jack Yeats paints
us, while bringing light

to our issueless existence
as only the great dare bring it,
reducing the dark where
mathematically at least,
there might have been a door . . .

Blue Infinity

Verlaine longed for a state
where nothing would "ruffle
or crease
this implacably smooth
horizon."

Was he guided by the same
nostalgia for azoic purity
that prompted Karl Popper
to say: "Matter
is a cancer in space"?

Paul Verlaine's original lines were "Rien qui plisse/ou ride cet
azur/implacablement lisse."

To Cézanne

How far you moved from Manet's
snapshot puerilities, from
Monet's superficial perceptions,
while still hailing the latter as
". . . an eye
though, by God, what an eye!"

First not to serve up pretty
pictures for the hiker's pleasure,
you soon understood the dynamic
intrusion to be yourself,
and landscapes mere
arrangements of atoms, patterns
we must mercilessly cast aside
in any attempt to reach
the essence of nature. Only then
were you able to take your great
leap forward

and with you, I shout, "To hell
with all this fucking scenery!"

The New Isn't

Walking, breathing in a new world,
why have I not found the end
of the old? Why can't I shed
its virus in my turds,
the *petites merdes* of my soul
palmed off on editors? It's not
as if it were single moments
unexpectedly slipping through
the gates. Those could be
dealt with, guarded against.
No, it's an almighty thumping,
relentless, inescapable
as a mother's heartbeat
to the child trapped in her womb.
Boom, boom. *Ta Gueule!*

. . . though it is too, the heavy
breathing of a bellows that keeps
alive the flame, if flame it is,
of my writing.

Baggage

Verbal baggage strangling
all attempts at thought,
can't write, can't imagine
even the shape of a sentence.

Wish to God I could shed
dead ideas as do ants
deciduous wings.
Futile to try and squeeze
out something new by force.
Only its own momentum
can make the outcome valid.
The act must be fluid,
instinctive as the opening
of one's mouth after
a near-drowning.

Little by Little

The needling hands
on my watch straddle time,
a double-headed monster,

spur it on
squeeze it
into a warp, smoke
it out, turn it
into a fourth dimension
ride it over stars, sail
it down galactic rivers
push it off
the world's edge

but, not done tormenting,
my watch ticks on.

"Little by little" is a quote from Endgame, *a late Beckett play.*

The Stake

Of the mother tongue, so aptly
named, every syllable pulls
and tugs till, desperate, you can
only think: Away!

away to another language
with no strings.
A clean break. That's far enough,
you think, enough is plenty

but find it isn't, for you go on
looking under the bed, outside
your door, scanning the night
beyond for freedom
like a goat still tied
to its stake though it has pulled
it up and now must drag it along
at every step.

If Sprung

from the soil
of a country named
on the map, tearing
out one's roots
gives exile
tangible substance

but if born
into a failure
of place, replacements
can never be more

and cuckoo-like
we carry on, though
subterraneous tugging
persists from both
non-places, can never
be stilled no matter
how often we say
"God bless!" and turn
away.

Walls

Since I paid homage
to Buddhism's striving
for the ablation of desire,
many find Zen or Taoist roots
in my work. I absolutely deny
this — though am curiously
pleased if, unbeknownst to me,
it is true . . .

yet wonder: can staring
at a wall lead to tranquility?
And was this achieved
by the Zen Master who cut
off his eyelids
not to fall asleep?

When I look at walls,
writing appears on them
compared to which
my own is a relief.

In the Beginning

nothing but leaf
on a reptile-ruled planet
when the first flower opened
and spread, "an abominable
mystery," Darwin said,
entirely avoidable. Evolution
was slower then, simpler too,
so little sex, scent
and hue not yet formulated,
nor beauty as a concept.

Did we wait somewhere
for that flower to blossom
and produce seed?
Or did it wait
for us to show
a need, the plant growing
for us and we for it
before sinning came
into the world
before desire
was born?

Out of the Primeval Soup
into the Frying Pan

You, Flaubert, stylist
par excellence, dreamt
of writing a book about nothing,
a book with no external support,
able to sustain itself
by the power of its style alone,
"as does the earth in mid-air."

Mid-air? What of gravity?
At the beginning, in the first
flush of puberty, the universe
gave intimate forces free-play
before, little by little,
gravity came to hold sway
in the primeval soup.

And now, without it, where
would we be? In fact,
we wouldn't.
It's an imperative
— the shattering, unbearable
gravity of being.

On Being

Gazing into the synaptic chasm
is to see the skull form
in the mother's womb, plates
of hard bone round
into shape, readied
to incarcerate a psyche
from the start condemned
to life without parole

. . . oh, to be able to see
instead a soap bubble
blown into existence
on a whim, delicate,
insubstantial, even beautiful
shimmering in sunlight until
suddenly, it is no more.

Mithradates

Who'd remember you now
had you killed one Roman,
but eighty thousand in a single
day made you a hero, assured
you a place in history and art
so too your tireless search
for a universal antidote,
fearing poisons above all.

Twenty-one hundred years later
we still have massacres,
search for antidotes, fear
is unabated, the entire
spectrum of human follies
but on we go, cling to soothing
old tales, the great words
repeated in the dark, over heads
of the newborn and bodies
of the dead on this grim
and touching bitch of an earth.

The legendary "Poison King," King Mithradates VI of Pontius (134–63 BC), creator of a formidable Black Sea empire was, until recently, one of the most celebrated figures of the classical world, a hero of opera, drama and poetry.

How History Works

On a May day in 1618, in a fight
over religion, two imperial regents
and their secretary were thrown out
of a window in Prague. All three
landed in a dung heap
and survived. Still, the act led
to a bloody thirty-year war.

Looking on the bright side,
the incident gave birth
to a grand word, "defenestration."
Also, we learned that dung heaps
have their uses.

Shakespeare Knew

A strange compulsion pushes me
into pursuing the worst. Always has.
As Lear says: "the worst is not
so long as one can say, 'This is
the worst.'"

If language, by definition, fails,
paring it down
to its absolute minimum
may be preferable.

My silences have always been wordy . . .
The attempt to do worse is doomed.
In reality, a writer
can only keep trying
"to fail better."

A Walk with Hippocrates

It's a millennium and a half
since you trod this earth
but I find myself conversing
with you as if you were walking
by my side along these French
country roads, and heard me pick
at your wisdom, mull over
your conclusions. Most cannot be
disputed — that opportunity
is fleeting, experience treacherous,
judgement difficult, life short, Yes
to all of these. But art, *long?*
Bear in mind, please, that some,
not unworthy, goes off
like fruit, the soft bits first,
so one must prune the work
to its pith, let it ring out clear
as does the cello, unaccompanied
but sufficient, in a Bach suite,
and hope the heavens will bend
down to listen before the wind
carries it off.

Homage to Montaigne

I see you in your tower where, four
hundred years ago, you sat and wondered,
"Was writing ever so prolific as since
the start of our civil wars? Had
the Romans ever written so much as just
before their collapse?" and concluded,
"Scribbling is but one symptom of an age
of excess!" Surely aware of the irony,
you said this after you'd holed up
in your tower with a chair, a table,
a thousand books and shut the door,
to reflect and scribble
for the next twenty years.

You read and wrote, wrote and read,
carved into the beams and woodwork
of your tower, your favourite quotes
— your preferred company,
for what could be pleasanter than
to have their authors speak to you
across millennia yet leave you alone,
giving you "scope and freedom" to think;
have them spring to life in your essays
and demolish one another's arguments?
No dogma was secure from the play
of your mind as you sat surrounded
by pagan friends whom you loved
and honoured but discarded

along with their congenial wisdom,
their comforting truths for, like
the skeptic, Sextus Empiricus,
you knew that truth is curved
and time itself a circle.

You acknowledge having gathered
garlands of other men's flowers,
"Nothing is mine but the cord
that binds them," but do not place
them on a pedestal, for every man bears
the whole stamp of the human condition,
— "kings and philosophers defecate,
and so do ladies."

You knew that one must go where
the silence is and say something,
expressed your horror at the barbarity
of the rack, of torture, chastizing
those who practised it in the name
of duty and religion — not even enemies
but fellow citizens!
With words that would bleed
were they cut, you evoke your father
and mourn your soul's friend.
If pressed as to why you loved him,
you said only: because he was he
and you were you.

It is with them you discuss death,
quoting Seneca, "To philosophize
is to learn to die." But getting
"lost in words and the gait of poetry"
put you off dying.

The entire cast of kings, statesmen,
historians, philosophers, poets,
saints and scoundrels from your books,
intrudes on your gloom, vies for your
attention and almost always wins.
How wonderfully human you are when
suddenly, your all-encompassing
interests change direction, to set
you pondering the vagaries of penises,
as you note, "the disobedience
of this member which thrusts itself
forward so inopportunely."

In your conversations you observed
the mind leaping ahead of its last
convictions, and end your essay
"On Vanity" with ancient Greece's
Delphic caveat, "Know thyself,"
turning vanity on its head as you urge
us to pursue the inner self, however
fractured, since there lies the only
path to real knowledge. Like Socrates,
you knew that to philosophize is not

to bludgeon your opponent
into accepting your views, but do
battle with yourself for, "of all
creatures, not one is as empty
and needy as man — he is the seeker
with no knowledge, the judge
with no jurisdiction,
the jester of the farce."

Single-handedly you brought into
the world a new spirit of criticism
and disillusionment affecting
every thinker from Shakespeare
and Bacon to Descartes, from Nietzsche
to Proust and Joyce. Without you,
where would our scribbling have been
in this new age of excess?

My dear friend, I will conclude
knowing you would wish me to tell you
how it is with us today and must confess
that the wrongs you observed have
multiplied a thousand fold, gaining
only in complexity.

Were you to hear of our condition,
of how we are snuffing the very earth
we stand on, you would be moved to tears
in whatever circle of heaven above
or Erebus below, you may be dwelling.
Farewell!

Doppelgänger

Success, failure — neither
matters. Never did! Still,
having breathed deep
of its vivifying air, failure
is what I feel most at home
with. Incongruous then
that people come now to consult
me, refuse a simple denial
of knowledge, question me
on how to live. *Me?*
They think me a soothsayer,
but I too am approaching
a fate beyond my comprehension
and, worse, am in perpetual
search of a place to put
my rage at life itself.

They come . . . and now,
grafted on to my roots, I feel
another me growing irresistibly,
an ageless pine splitting
a rock to forge ahead
no matter the cost. This other,
is he still me? Living
by my rules? And were he not
bedevilled by my despair,
my frustrations, the ballast
that keeps me afloat, might
he too, be as lost
as would Goethe's Young Werther
without his sorrows?

Murphy, the protagonist in Beckett's novel by that name, owes an "indefinable something" to Goethe's The Sorrows of Young Werther.

Le Rêve d'Alembert

How apt your meditation on
the beginning of the living world,
my dear Diderot, and with what
an astonishing mental leap
you anticipated the doctrine
of survival by the fittest
— a daring and irreligiousness
that soon had you imprisoned
and your *Pensées philosophiques*
burned publicly —

nor did our dependence on
sense perception escape you,
how the blind might read
by touch, and the deaf and dumb
still benefit from the aesthetic
of language — of all things!

an anaesthetic?

Beckett much admired the writing of Denis Diderot (1700–1784) and drew on Le Rêve d'Alembert *for his own* Dream.

The Senses

Don't Jung's concentric spheres
— light, half-light and dark —
mirror the three realms
of the Buddhist cosmos
where all five senses
are present in the first; taste,
smell and touch are absent
from the second and the third
has only mind — that Jungian
centre, his *dark zone*?

True, mind *is*
but what of mind's heart?
It too *is*
panting and bleeding, clenching,
unclenching, its groaning
weight drags us under
the swollen surface
into the unquiet belly
of strutting, fretting life.

Beckett structured his first novel, Murphy, *on Jung's image of three concentric spheres.*

Galileo Galilei

First to see the skies clearly
through your telescope
you soon proved Copernicus
right: Earth does indeed
revolve around the sun
and not vice versa. But oh,
what hackles you raised
among the faithful
for unseating us
from our throne in the universe!
Charged with "vehement suspicion
of heresy," did you cross
your fingers behind your back
while you recanted
before the Roman Inquisition,
"I abjure, curse and detest
my past errors"?

You were the first to perceive
that math and physics link
celestial and terrestrial
realities, and so destroyed
the division between the world
above and the world
below the moon;

first to discover Jupiter's
satellites; the phases of Venus;
the moon's uneven surface;

first to see that even the sun
has spots.

When the Chief Priests

had delivered Jesus to Pilate,
Pilate asked him, "Art thou the King
of the Jews?" And he answered,
"Thou sayest it." And the chief
priests accused him of many things
but he answered nothing.
And Pilate asked him again,
saying, "Answerest thou
nothing? Behold how many things
they witness against thee."
But Jesus yet answered nothing
so that Pilate marvelled.

Had He recanted . . .

What Is This

hovering in spaces
between things, between
cultures, languages,
past and future,
suspended between
knowledge and the lack
of it, neither innocent
nor guilty?

"Ah, the old questions,
the old answers!"
Such a comfort.

The Scream

I'm bursting with Munch,
Shostakovich tugs
at my seams while Picasso's
white dove has wings
smeared with oil.

Alfred Nobel, a lonely man,
invented dynamite, then,
sitting on a keg of it,
bequeathed a Peace Prize.
Was his sleep henceforth
less troubled? Perhaps
not, for there followed
his wife's affair
with a mathematician.
Peaceful by nature,
he shied away from
explosives, from fuses,
wanted no fuss or mess,
simply decreed that all
sciences receive awards
— except mathematics.

Music

Rachmaninoff's chords ranged
and arranged, become pyramids
— no: mountains! Warts
on the earth, so much larger
than we are, in excess
of what we are

while Bach's outpourings
are masonry built
on certainties
of which there are none!
As for Mahler or Wagner —
heaven help us!

Ah, for the simplicity
of Schubert lieder, the song
and its accompaniment entering
one another deeply, to be less,
to throw only one shadow,
the sound reduced to a single
cry of sorrow and desolation
so profound it overwhelms.

Denting the Dark

Voices, snatches
of conversation, bats
in the night, flap around
me in the dark.
Silence! I say.
Order in my thoughts!

Allow peace for visual
fragments sliding quietly
into place, to lasso
a meaning on the wing
so the image that emerges
can illumine
an infinitesimal moment
in our space-time
on this side of nothing

— the most we may hope for.

Atlas

This all-consuming drive
to perform a task, albeit
self-imposed, before
I can end — leave no silence
unturned, uncover the worms
through a tortuous exercise
as if my life depended
on it even as I reject it
as if I were a schoolboy
in detention forced to write
penal lines though no one
compels me to,
but speak I must before
I am done.

To console myself
with a mission? Feel part
of an uncomprehending world
that moves between
a beginning and an end
shamming logic?

Then why do I hear myself sound
like Schubert's wretched Atlas
condemned to bear alone
all the world's unbearable pain?

4th September 1939

Learning that "Kol Nidre"
is the title of a prayer sung
on the eve of atonement,
for a moment replaced
in my mind "Cooldrinagh"
name of my home,

atonement: for being lured
by the maternal trap
while obsessed by the urge
to escape, at each homecoming
determined to leave again
at once but always waiting
for the point of desperation
when nothing could hold me.

No waiting this time
— France at war!
Must head back to Paris
at once.
The world, at its worst
at its best also,
throbs godlessly.

"Cooldrinagh" is Irish for "back of the blackthorn hedge."

War Zone 1944

Blasted walls, twisted metal.
Remnants of houses, whipped
by wind and rain. In one,
a father's feet have worn
away the surface of the lino,
shuffling to and fro in front
of his chair, to and fro,
while he listens to Radio Free
Europe, gets up to move
tiny flags marking Allied
and Axis positions on the map
stuck to the wall, sits again
and shuffles, his child bent
over homework, drawing
the country's outline,
small fingers blackening
the border to make it thick,
safe, the spitting and crackle
of wet logs in the stove
echoing distant intermittent
gunfire, the shuffle
of the father's feet,
the swishing through mud
of army boots.

"Minari" — Latin for "to Threaten"

from the Indo-European
root "men" that gave us "menace,"
"mouth" . . .

mouths threatening
everywhere,
thirsty, devouring,
screaming,
unstoppable, a dull
roar in the skull.

Skulls were the Vikings'
drinking cups.

One day the earth
will be a skull
raised to whose lips?

St.-Lô

Shells of buildings, forlorn,
ghostly, in a sea of mud, no
water, no sanitation . . .
rebuild — what first?
what second?
hospitals? people?
numbers interwoven
with the numberless

must the word
they've acted on
be cut from the tongues
of our workforce,
these prisoners in muddy
blood-splattered boots,
then emptiness
be carved into their souls?

Everywhere the forgotten
are groping to forget,
fragmented body parts,
earth parts, swim together,
hearts too, fragmented,
and minds, see nothing
ahead, nothing behind
taste only the ashes
of loss.

In 1944 St.-Lô was named "La Capitale des Ruines" *by journalists. In 1945
Beckett worked there with an Irish unit of the Red Cross.*

1945

Step warily, it's different
from what you think,
what I think: secrets still
live not just in eyes,
still throw shadows

faces drained of colour
spell it out,
thin faces, bent
bodies walk as if
carrying a corpse
under the heart.

So this is peace.
Can love return
to beds?

Confrontation

I see it coming, the eye
the seeing I, coming closer

not in a Rembrandt way, not
with paint folded and creased
into the face; with tear ducts,
a dribble of impasto; tendrils
of hair etched into still wet paint,
pigment smeared and smudged
with fingers to give
the tangible surface of life

but as Felix Nussbaum did,
painting himself in a Belgian attic
while hiding from the Nazis,
a self-portrait that shows him
wearing the yellow Star of David
on his coat and, in his hand,
holding an ID card that says
"JUIF — JOOD," though he'd never
worn the yellow Star nor possessed
this ID card. He was on the run,
pretending not to be Jewish
but even as he ran, needed
to see, to confront
his worst fears before
being hunted down
and sent to Auschwitz.

Day In, Day Out

facing those caged
like animals in the Prison
de la Santé, across the street
from me, I think of the one
finally caught, finally tried,
finally hanged in that yard,
whose death I cannot
mourn (though unable to take
even the life of the rat
I saved from my Maquis
comrades' guns)

the one who falsely heard
the confessions of those whose
cell he'd infiltrated, whose
confidence he'd gained to betray
to the Gestapo, who were beaten,
tortured, killed, good men
and brave. Their crime? Trying
to thwart the Nazi occupiers
as *he* pretended to, or simply
the shape of their noses

killed as we would have been
had we not been warned in time
to run to freedom

freedom to sit here now, to look
at hands clutching the bars
of those cells and listen
to the inmates' shouts,
their wailing and clamouring;
freedom to suffer with them.

Some wonder why, in my plays,
I have not used this setting
so conveniently there
for me, across from
my very house, don't see
there's no need: all of us
are behind invisible bars
and life itself a cage.

Robert Alesch, a French priest who infiltrated Gloria SMH, the Resistance cell to which Beckett belonged, and betrayed its members to the Gestapo, was hanged at the Prison de la Santé. From the studio of his house, Beckett could see this prison. Using a mirror, he sometimes communicated with one of the prisoners in Morse code.

Gore

Keeping one's mouth shut
is not enough.

Like the starfish
that quickly inserts its stomach
into a tiny opening
of the oyster's shell
then digests it

the media insert a camera.

Entanglement

Held by gravity on an insignificant
speck among trillions, aware that
bacteria live happily in boiling
water kilometres below our feet,
that we're not what we seem
but may consist of microscopic
building blocks — tiny vibrating
"strings" in a space-time
of ten dimensions when
we cannot even cope with three;
that well over ninety percent
of the universe is in some
mysterious, invisible form
whose horrors we cannot fathom

but know that particles have
telepathy, are able to sense
one another and even when
widely separated, behave as if
intimately connected.

It's more than we can
even in proximity.

At the Corner of
Boulevard Blanqui, Paris

"Ben, alors! A nous deux!"
Sure the gruff voice is challenging
me — it has happened before on
a Paris street — I look up, but no,
the man, bottle clutched in left
hand, is addressing a cock
teetering on his forearm, its feet
clawing his bare skin as it slithers
and slides, comb flopping, eye
bleary, beak dipping
into the glass he proffers
with his right, wine glinting
ruby in a stray ray of light,

man and bird oblivious
to sudden ominous skies
and the disquiet soon to descend
on those who lack an adversary.

Oblivious, oh Lord, how long?

"Ben, alors! A nous deux!" *translates from French to "Right then!*
It's us two now!"

Incoherent State

Is mathematics a construct
or discovery? We can't tell
but some live for numbers,
dream numbers, get drunk
on numbers, celebrate
Archimedes' pi approximation
and fail to see that all
of life is an approximation.

There is something about order
about equations and symmetry
that appeals and consoles
if you are horribly alone,
like a heaven-sent ladder
when you've fallen down a hole,
even if you cannot reach it
just counting the rungs
could save your sanity.

Waiting for Godot

What a free-for-all this play
has led to — with no end in sight.
The questions, "Why the wait?"
and "Who is he?"
have numberless minds mulling
over countless possible answers
— some quite intriguing —
when there obviously are none.

All I claim is to present
the way it is:
most can only wait
and yes, some serve.

Not I

It hardly showed in all that
grey, having assumed the colour
of asphalt — for safety,
its upper body raised on front
legs, abdomen and hind legs
flattened by a passing car,
the chameleon stood, barely,
in the middle of the road
not knowing it was a road
or where roads lead or why
it had led him to this,
its jaw opening and closing,
excruciatingly silent.

Could one stage a mouth?
A moving mouth, visceral,
the rest of the face hidden
in darkness, gaping
at an audience, working
on their nerves
not their intellect,
language not there
but insinuated
by the spotlighted image.
They may not react any more
than did passers-by
to the chameleon,
but can they forget it?

Not I *is the title of a Samuel Beckett play in which a moving mouth is featured as a character.*

Rasch und mit Feuer

No need to show this triangle in all
its banality, only the emotional state
of the three characters, their minds
exploding in chaos, raging on
as though what triggered it
were not long past, the rage
repeating itself endlessly, the event
living on in their heads, the man,
his wife and his mistress obsessively
chewing on it. A short one-act,
titled *Play*. Spoken very quickly,
almost incomprehensibly fast,
gathering momentum. Certain syllables
stressed, relished,
used for rhythmic purpose.

Three characters who, like three
members of a string quartet, speak only
when the fourth — a spotlight — shines
on each in turn, prodding them to life,
but stop short when it moves on.
The spotlight, erratic, will not wait
for the speaker to complete a sentence,
before turning to another. Repeat
the entire text at the end? Beethoven
would. In a different order? Perhaps.

Though plucked from life, it will
make no sense. Reality never
does. I'll say so in the text.
Yes, I'll insert the line,
"Pardon, no sense in this,
oh, I know — "
That, dear critics, is my response
to you, ever ready to misconstrue,
no matter how often I repeat to all
and sundry: it means simply
what it says. No more, no less.

But I'll be miserly with the bare
bones I cast abroad.

Rasch und mit Feuer *is a German musical term meaning "fast and with passion." Beckett conceived his plays as pieces of music, with rhythm and tempo all-important components.*

Ghost Trio

How few are left buried deep
in the tundra of your sadness
of the great loves you have
known. Others, once
passionately desired,
have vanished
without trace along with
the old fear of the dark

but there is one, perfectly
preserved in the frozen subsoil
of those wastes, whose laughter
still echoes in yours,
who may stir
among the mosses, the stunted
shrubs and lichens
and invade your whole being,
suddenly brought to life
on hearing a certain pause
in Beethoven's *Ghost Trio*

a deep pause once shared.

The Good

That ant hastening slowly
along its path, bearing
a seed three times
its own size for the good
of the ant heap
the good of the queen
doesn't know it can't
think: "I can't
go on." Just goes on.

Footfalls

will do as title, hints at ghostly
steps. Only one actress will be
on stage. The focal point must be how
she holds herself, how she moves
to express the inexpressible.

Old before her time, I see her
going back and forth on a threadbare
strip of carpet as if caged
in its two dimensions, unable to break
out of her rut — seven paces to the left,
wheel, seven to the right, wheel, talking
all the while. With a mother? Yes.
An invalid mother who shall remain
invisible, whose voice, real or not,
occupies her mind, her poor mind.
Best have it come from off-stage.
Tempo ever-decreasing in an inverted
danse macabre, while she diminishes,
folds into herself, toward gradual
nothingness, not yet completely
gone but no longer quite there. Finally,
an illusion created by lighting, not
of a figure, but a tangle of grey tatters
vanishing, stunning onlookers. But oh,
Lord, what will it do to the actress?

Footfalls *is the title of a Beckett play.*

Winterreise

Ironic? These poems? Schubert clearly
thought not, nor can I, shivering
through this non-journey, feeling
we are one, the wanderer and I,
on a snowy road out of a village
where his love spurned him, under
a spinning weathervane, the landscape
vague. Tears freeze on his cheeks,
he searches for her footprints,
looks at words of love
he once carved into the linden.

Below its crust of ice, a flowing
river is a heart beating in a cold
body. The post horn's calls raise
hopes for a letter but I — no: he
has no address. A fluttering leaf
appears to hold fate in the balance.

Back in the village, dogs rattle
their chains, bark at us,
a crow harasses us, impatient
for us to be corpses.
But lamenting is for fools!
In a burst of courage we walk
on though mock suns in the sky
make us long for night.

Careful to avoid signposts, we chance
on a graveyard — inn of eternal rest,
but there is no vacancy.
His plate empty, an organ grinder,
fellow outcast, is playing
a tune for no one.

With rambling tempo, chords
and obstinate note patterns
repeated, we're still on the same
road, leaving the same village
nowhere-bound, not surrendering
to loneliness, but letting it cut
more deeply, letting it
ferment and season.

Winterreise *is a song cycle by Schubert, which Beckett found deeply affecting.*

Truth Decay

To write a play, not about
something, but itself something
takes language free of prior sense
. . . alas, all man has touched
is contaminated.
Giving up hope for meaning
— much as I crave it and abhor
hopelessness — is the only way.

Is all I produce maniacally
inconclusive? But life is no
less so. I do my best, give
the work symmetry, balance
grief and rage with comedy,
the yearning for expression
tempered by knowing
that language betrays truth.
That, my friends, is why
not one of my characters stands
on a rug that can't be pulled
out from under him.

For all my exploitation
of absurdities, life looks no less
absurd. But surely you hear me
with Hamm and all the others,
cry "No!" to nothingness?

Hamm is the principal character in Beckett's play Endgame.

What Is This

stuff we're made of
that allows neutrinos
not only to bombard us
but pass through us
in their hundreds
of billions — by day
from above, at night
from below
while the sun hides
behind the world?

as if we didn't have
enough to cope with!

Ellipse with Two Foci

We are two, he and I,
he so busy rebraiding
himself for the daily slog,
conventions, duties,
even relationships

he remains unaware of the I
whose life runs in a secret
parallel until he suddenly
discovers it, sees
it's the repository
of the sacred, the meaningful
and knows there is no longer
the strength or will
to go on with both

but not to worry, the mind
has already begun to shed
its outer layers, tighten
its belt, cut back
on its appetite
and the I is saved.

Like Water

. . . we flow, go
underground
in the dark, clash
with obstacles, follow
curves, deepen
hollows, keep moving
forward, willy-nilly
forward, all the while
straining back
to recall some
thing some one
making it up maybe
to stop the void
from pressing in

always forward and down
over the fall
ahead.

Wordlessly

How far the journey
from those early pieces laced
with daylight, eager expectation
and soon the temerity to address
Napoleon — by then traitor
to earlier ideals — "You are
fortunate that I am not a general,
for I would defeat you!"

to several lifetimes later
after total deafness
and disillusion had brought
much bile to bottle
in the major works
but none is trapped there.
Instead came deeper music,
wordlessly eloquent.

More life passed, and strife,
before late Beethoven, no salt
dome, but wise, tightly focused
so that in the blackness
of pain, of deep anguish
and resignation, each exquisite
note becomes a candle.

The Tempest

Ah, Shakespeare, you were not Ariel
come to fly, to swim, to dive
into the fire, but more
of an all-seeing Prospero
who embraced his murky side
yet with bleak compassion
observed the poor forked creature
whose reason is so quickly undone
by desire.

Marooned for a lifetime
on this "bare island," earth
or stage, but really the world
of the imagination,
along with Prospero, about
to relinquish his magical powers,
you take your bow. "Every third
thought shall be of my grave,"
you say together in one voice.
"Our revels now are ended."
The creative bubble cannot
keep death at bay forever.

If one but could, like you, say
no more and still speak volumes

Hanging On

Now that every shift
in the weather ripples
through my aching body
— *das arme Tier* — memories
rise at my slightest
movement like roused flies
from a corpse. Good!
I think, best to banish
them, to knock out
the stuffing, strip
down to bare bones

then catch myself
reaching out
to hang on to one,
just one, I tell myself,
but struggle on
to recapture another
and another
too precious to lose.

Das arme Tier *translates from German to "that wretched creature."*

Tempus Edax Rerum

that's *not* how it feels when
you're young and miserable,
covered with boils and cysts,
drowning in anxiety, sleeping ten
hours at a stretch and wishing it
were twenty, worshipping
Schopenhauer who said sleep
is a death wish, convinced
his intellectual justification
of unhappiness is the greatest
ever, as life stretches before you
mercilessly, no rescue in sight
and, at each awakening, you feel
more like Job not complaining
to an invisible God but cursing
the day you were born when
you never asked to be, never given
a choice — what a choice! — made
to feel ungrateful even selfish,
for God's sake, because of
the clarity of vision that soon
you begin to lose, for nothing
lasts, but one fine day imagine,
try to imagine that all
this will end, all

and suddenly you do feel grateful
for being part of the process.

Tempus edax rerum *translates from Latin to "Time, devourer of all things."*

How Will it Be?

Will someone one day
speak of my mouth
not opening
or opening
and not speaking
or speaking
but not opening?

Comment ce sera-t-il?

Quelqu'un dira-t-il
un jour de ma bouche
qu'elle ne s'ouvre pas
ou qu'elle s'ouvre
mais ne parle pas
ou qu'elle parle
mais ne s'ouvre pas?

SUGGESTED FURTHER READING

Ackerley, C.J. & S.E Gontarski. *The Grove Companion to Samuel Beckett.* Grove Press, 2004.

Atik, Anne. *Comment c'était.* Editions de l'Olivier, 2003.

Bair, Deirdre. *Samuel Beckett.* Summit Books, 1978.

Cronin, Anthony. *Samuel Beckett.* Harper Collins, 1997.

Dukes, Gerry. *Samuel Beckett, Illustrated Lives.* Penguin, 2001.

Fehsenfeld, Martha Dow & Lois More Overbeck, editors. *The Letters of Samuel Beckett.* Cambridge University Press, 2009.

Kennedy, Seán, editor. *Beckett in Ireland,* Cambridge University Press, 2010.

Kenner, Hugh. *Samuel Beckett: A Critical Study.* Grove Press, 1961.

Knowlson, James. *Damned to Fame.* Grove Press, 1996.

Whitelaw, Billie. *Who He?* St. Martin's Press, 1996.

ABOUT THE AUTHOR

Born in Germany, Inge Israel grew up in France and Ireland and lived in Denmark for some years before settling in Canada. The recipient of several literary prizes and awards, and named Chevalier de l'Ordre des Arts et des Lettres, Israel is the author of eight books of poetry and short stories in French and English, essays and several plays. She now makes her home in Victoria, British Columbia.

RECYCLED
Paper made from
recycled material
FSC® C021757

Marquis Book Printing Inc.

Québec, Canada
2011

Printed on Silva Enviro 100% post-consumer EcoLogo certified paper,
processed chlorine free and manufactured using biogas energy.